MORRIS GOLDENBERG
SNARE DRUM
for beginners

containing
Basic Rudiments for Orchestral Drummers
Twenty-four Exercises for the Student
Twenty-four Duets for Student & Teacher

Copyright © 1970 by Chappell & Co., Inc.
International Copyright Secured   Printed in U.S.A.
ALL RIGHTS RESERVED

CHAPPELL MUSIC COMPANY

Introduction

It is my intention to provide in this book those Rudiments which I feel are basic to orchestral and ensemble playing. There are many other Rudiments for the drummer which are easily available in publications devoted exclusively to them. Rudiments are the basic exercises and studies for strengthening both hands, especially the weaker one, since they require the same precision from each. Rudiments will also improve the reflexes and develop a rapid stick technique. Among the Rudiments, the roll is the most important of all and will require more time to master it than the others.

In drumming, the motion of the sticks should be straight up and down, remembering that the shortest distance between two points is a straight line. The sticks should form an angle of app. 45° with the tips of the stick together, thus —

The duets will provide opportunity for the student to improve his reading ability and develop ensemble awareness. The new elements of each exercise are developed in the following duet and can serve as a test of how much the student has absorbed.

With the exception of contest solos, rendering of cadences for marching bands and during practice sessions, the use of the drums is rarely isolated from other pitched instruments. Drums are essential to most concerted instrumental music ranging from concert orchestra to marching, concert and stage bands and contemporary chamber music including the percussion ensemble. In the twentieth century, the drummer has become an indispensible part of the music scene.

— Morris Goldenberg

Rudiments

Each Rudiment should be practiced at least one minute daily and longer if necessary.

4

1. Exercise

Using quarter notes (♩) and quarter rests (𝄽).
Students should count: 1 - 2 - 1 - 2 aloud throughout the lesson.

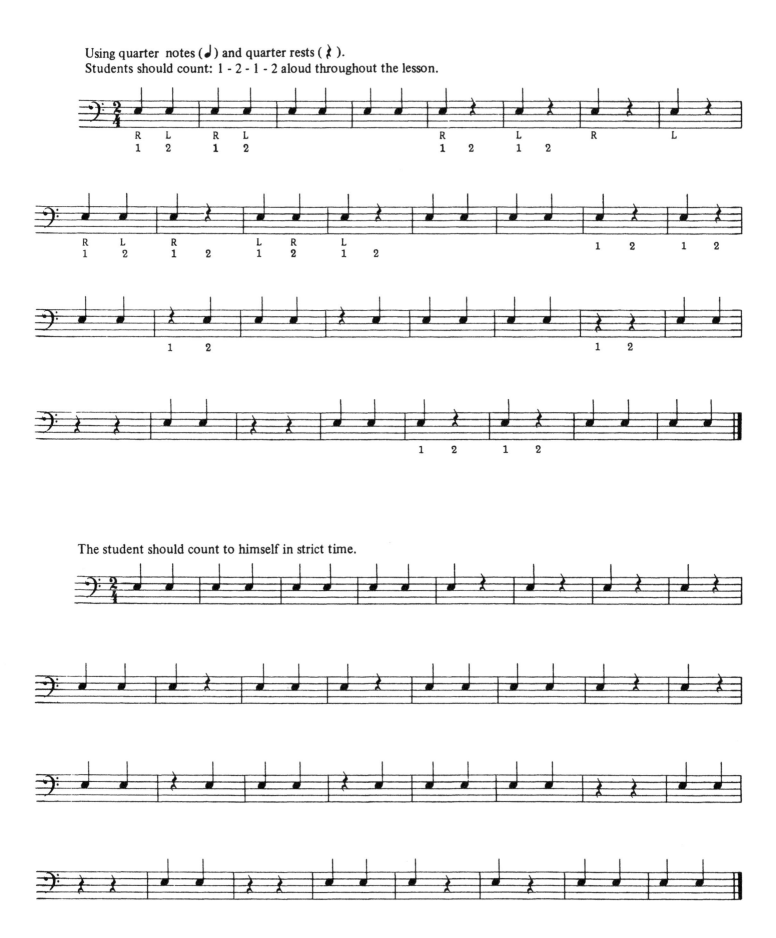

The student should count to himself in strict time.

1. Duet

Student

Teacher

2. Exercise in ¾ Time

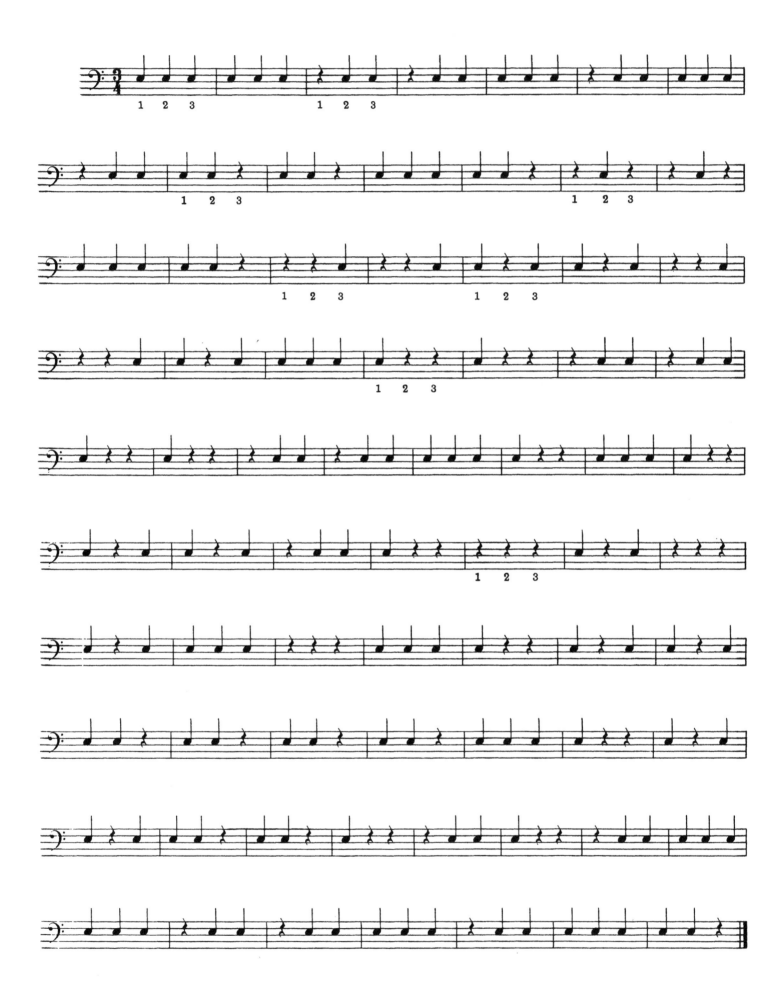

2. Duet in $\frac{3}{4}$

3. Exercise in 4/4 Time

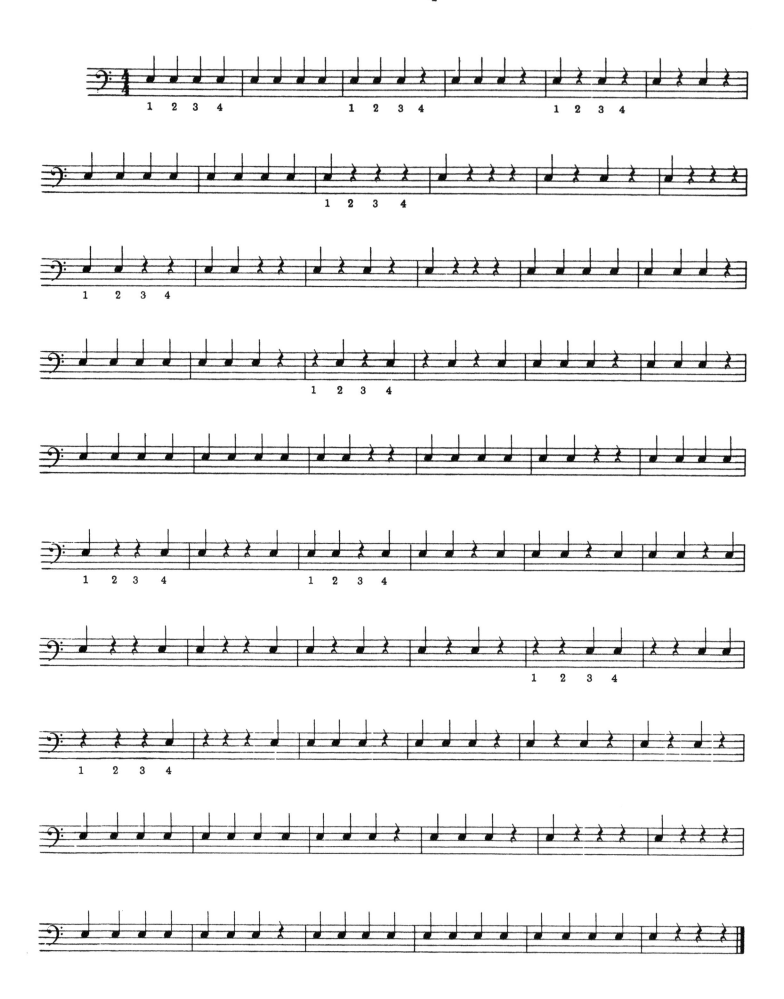

3. Duet in 4/4

4. Exercise with Eighth Notes (♪) and Eighth Rests (𝄾)

4. Duet in $\frac{2}{4}$ Time

12

5. Exercise with Quarter (♩) and Eighth Notes (♪)

5. Duet in $\frac{3}{4}$ Time

6. Exercise with Half Notes (♩) and Half Rests (▬)

6. Duet in 4/4

7. Exercise with Sixteenth Notes (♪) and Repeat Signs

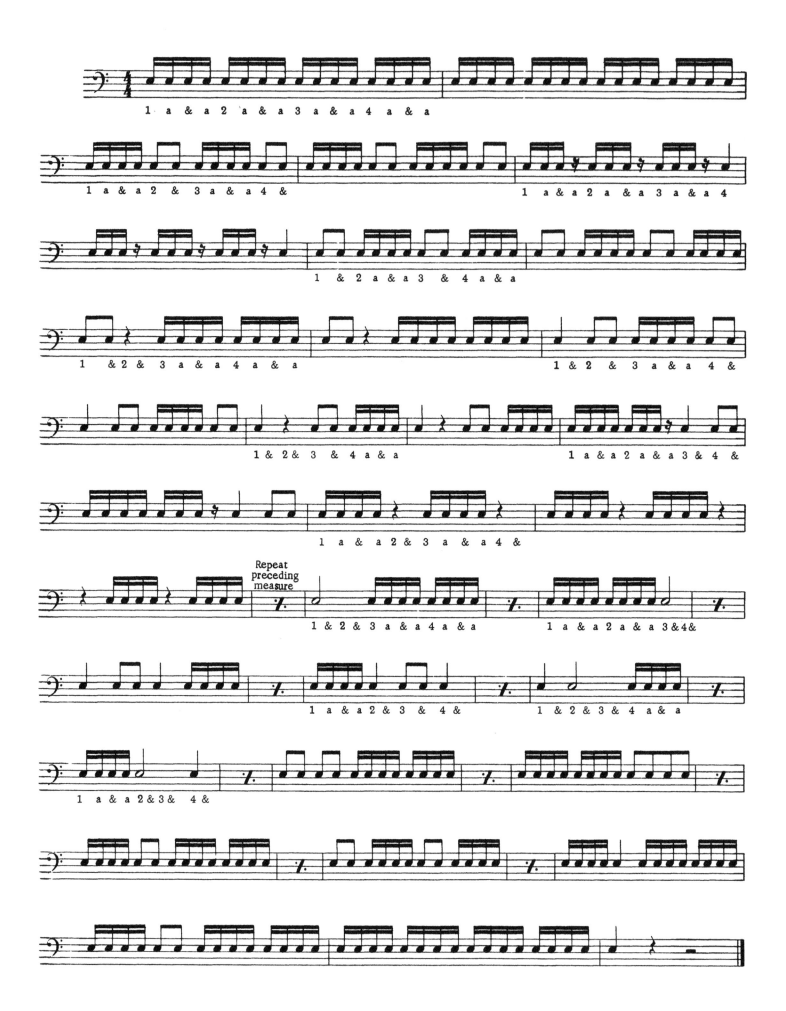

7. Duet in 4/4 with Sixteenth Rests (𝄾)

8. Exercise in 3/4 with Sixteenth Notes (♪) and Rests (𝄾)

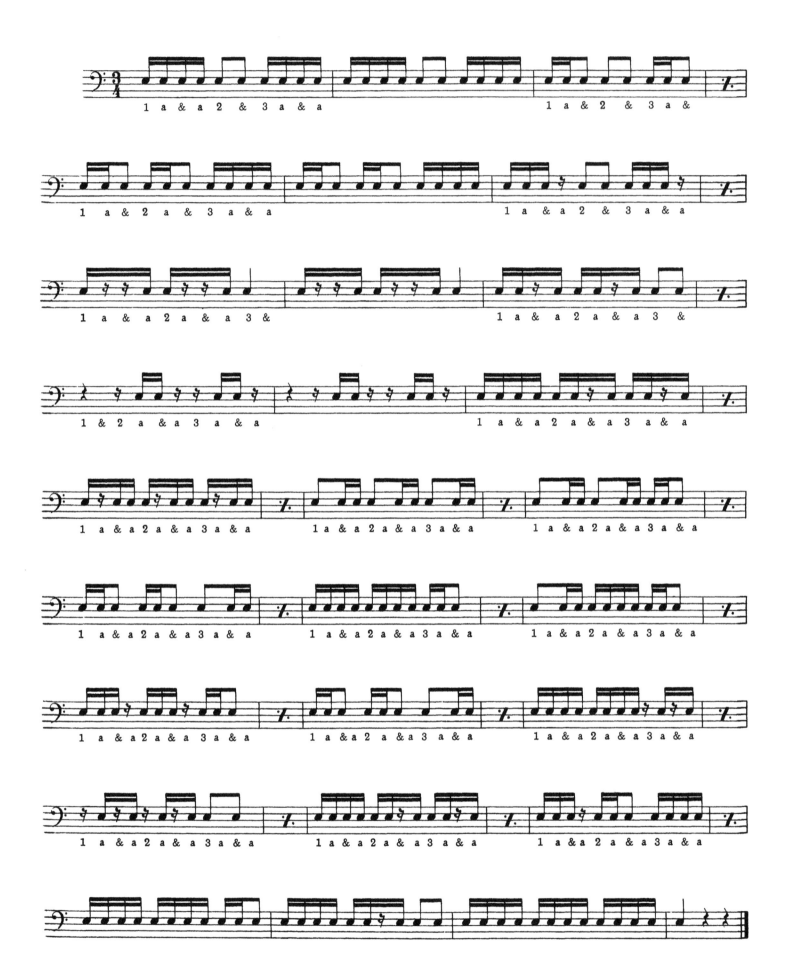

8. Duet in 3/4

9. Exercise in 3/4

9. Syncopated Duet in $\frac{3}{4}$

10. Exercise with Dotted Notes and Dotted Rests

A Dot (.) after a note adds ½ the value to the note before it. For instance, a quarter note with the dot (♩.) has the value of a quarter and an eighth. A dotted eighth note (♪.) has the value of an eighth and a sixteenth. The same applies to rests, dotted quarter (𝄽•) and dotted eighth (𝄾•). The Exercises below and on the following pages are good examples.

10. Duet in 4/4 Time

1 & 2 a & a 3 & 4 a & a   1 a & a 2 a & a 3 a & a 4 a & a

11. Exercise in $\frac{2}{4}$

11. Duet in 2/4

12. Exercise in 4/4

12. Duet in 4/4

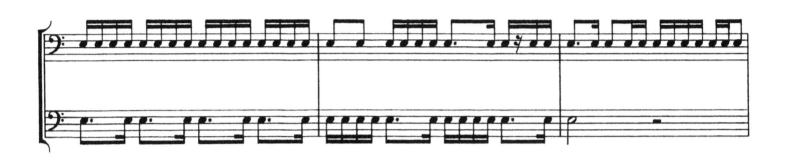

13. Exercise in $\frac{3}{4}$ Using Flams

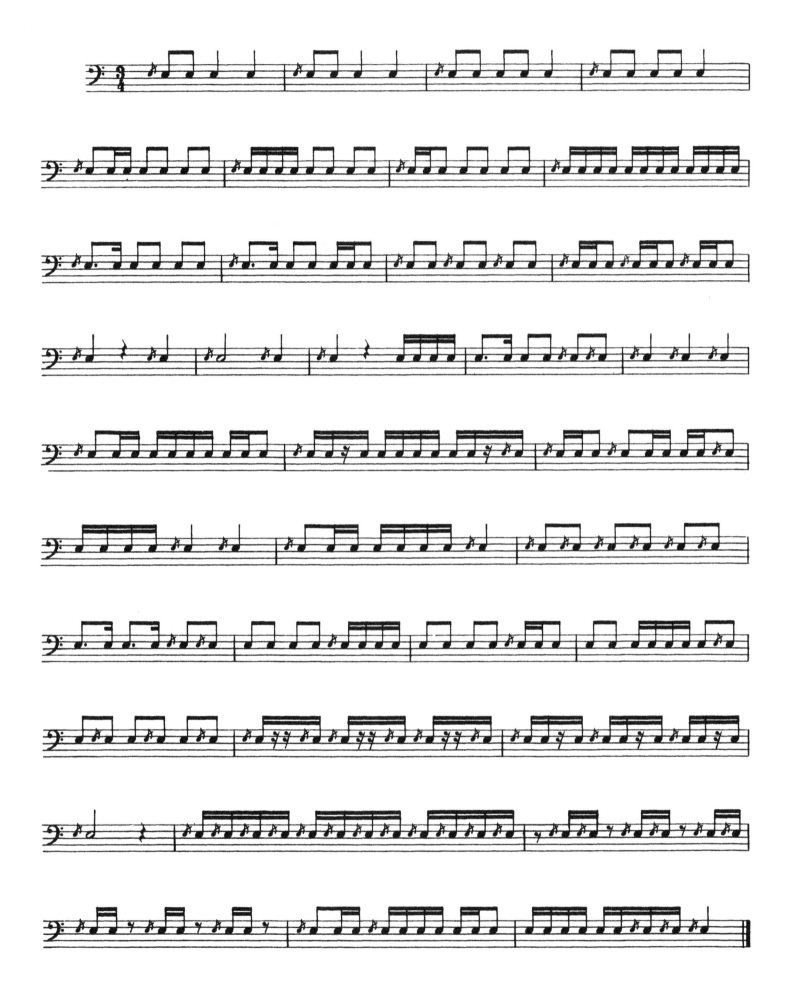

13. Duet in ¾

14. Review Exercise

Using all rhythms and note values studied

14. Duet in 4/4

15. Using Syncopated Patterns

15. Duet in 2/4

The Tied Note (♩♩): Notes tied together (⌣) (⌢) become one continuous Note. For example ♩♩ sounds like ♩ ; ♫♫ will be played the same as ♩ ♩ . Only the first note is attacked.

16. Exercise Introducing Ties

Eighth Note Ties

16. Tied Note Duet

17. Exercise

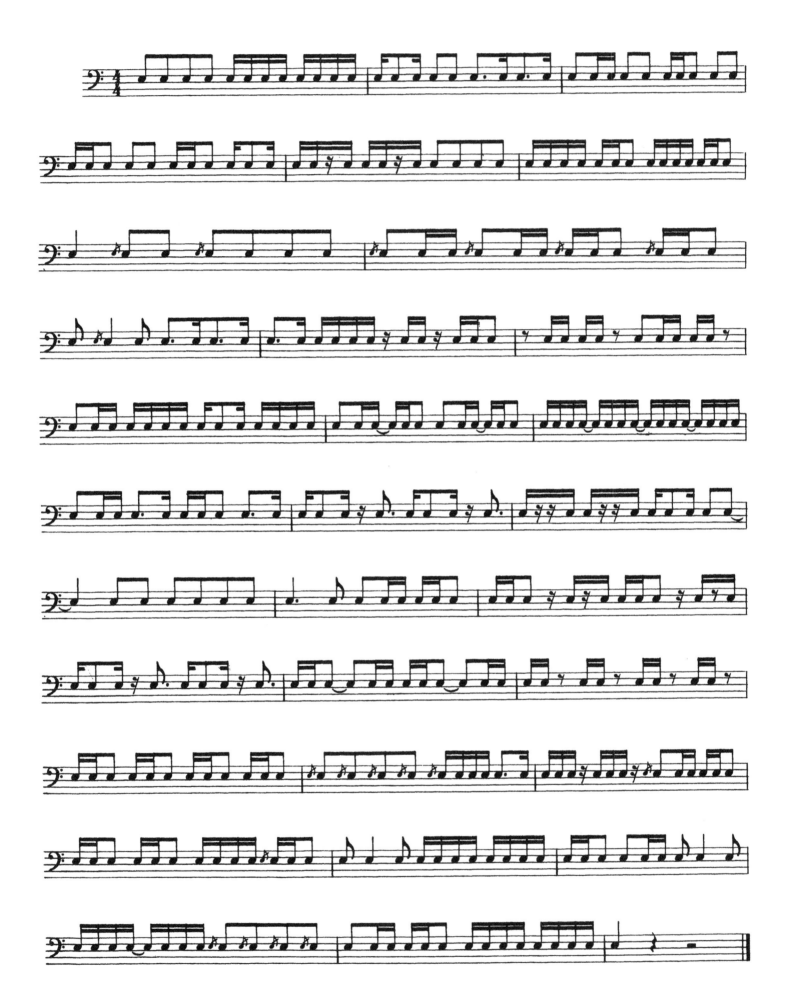

17. Duet

18. Exercise in $\frac{3}{4}$

18. Duet in ¾

19. Exercise Using Triplets

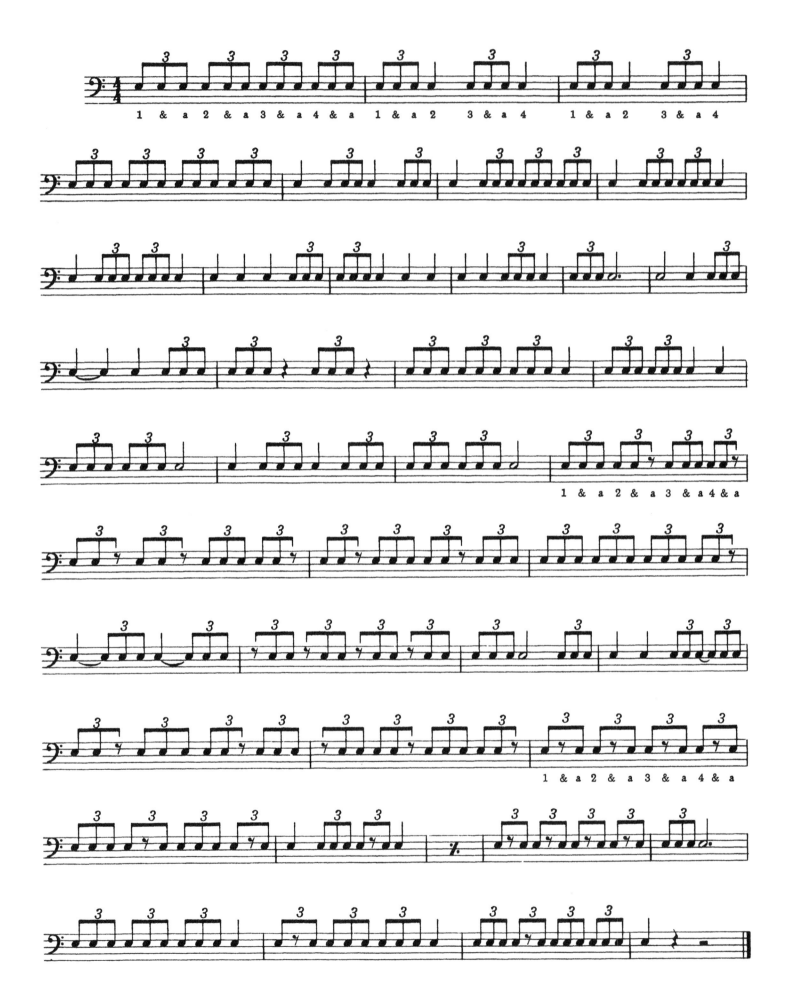

19. Duet in 4/4

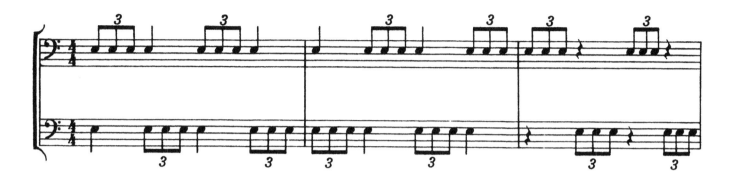

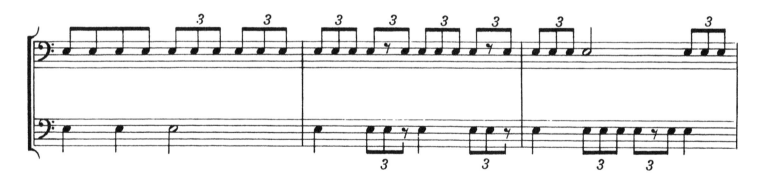

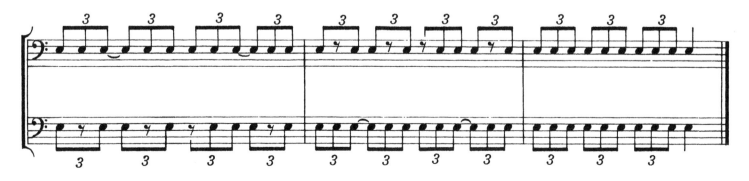

20. Review Exercise

20. Duet in $\frac{4}{4}$

21. Exercise Using the Eighth Note as the Basic Pulse

21. Duet in 3/8

46

22. Exercise in 3/8

22. Duet in $\frac{3}{8}$

23. Exercise in $\frac{3}{8}$ Using Triplets

23. Duet with Triplets

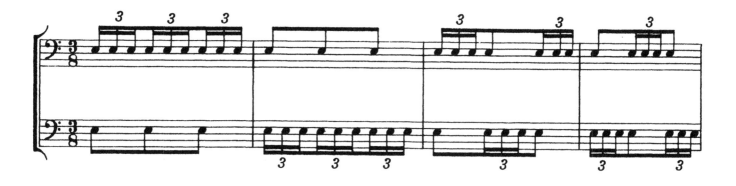

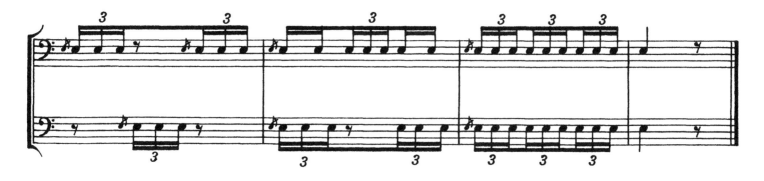

24. Exercise in 6/8

24. Duet in $\frac{6}{8}$

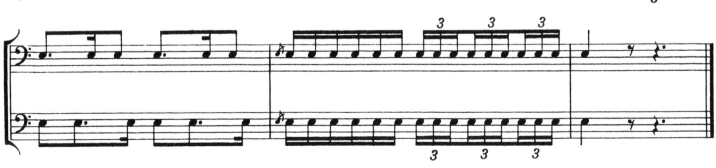

MORRIS GOLDENBERG, artist-percussionist and teacher, has long felt the need for a collection of standard orchestral literature which would supplement the basic timpani methods already available. This desire has culminated in a series: CLASSIC OVERTURES FOR TIMPANI, CLASSIC SYMPHON-IES FOR TIMPANI, ROMANTIC SYMPHONIES FOR TIMPANI, and STANDARD CONCERTOS FOR TIMPANI. The pages of all four books are reproduced from the standard editions used by every symphony orchestra. The student who studies these parts will become familiar with the appearance of the profes-sional timpanist's library, and will never have to unlearn what he has already accomplished. In selecting the works to be included in these volumes, Mr. Goldenberg always consid-ered the unique role the timpani part plays in each composi-tion and the unusual demands made on the player by the composer.

Morris Goldenberg is the author of several books for the per-cussion student and performer, "MODERN SCHOOL FOR XYLOPHONE . . ." and "MODERN SCHOOL FOR SNARE DRUM . . ." which are used as audition materials by all sym-phony orchestras and are required by the Royal Academy of Music in England. Also, Mr. Goldenberg has written the first method for training the percussionist on multiple instru-ments, "STUDIES IN SOLO PERCUSSION." The latter has been hailed as the "best" in its field and a "must for every serious percussionist."

Mr. Goldenberg is a staff percussionist at the NBC television studios in New York. In addition to his many recording and performing commitments, the author is a faculty member of the Juilliard School of Music where he has trained orchestral musicians since 1941.